AF428012

What's so Special About a Tree?

For Daddy, who would have gotten a
kick out of creating a book with me

What's so Special About a Tree?

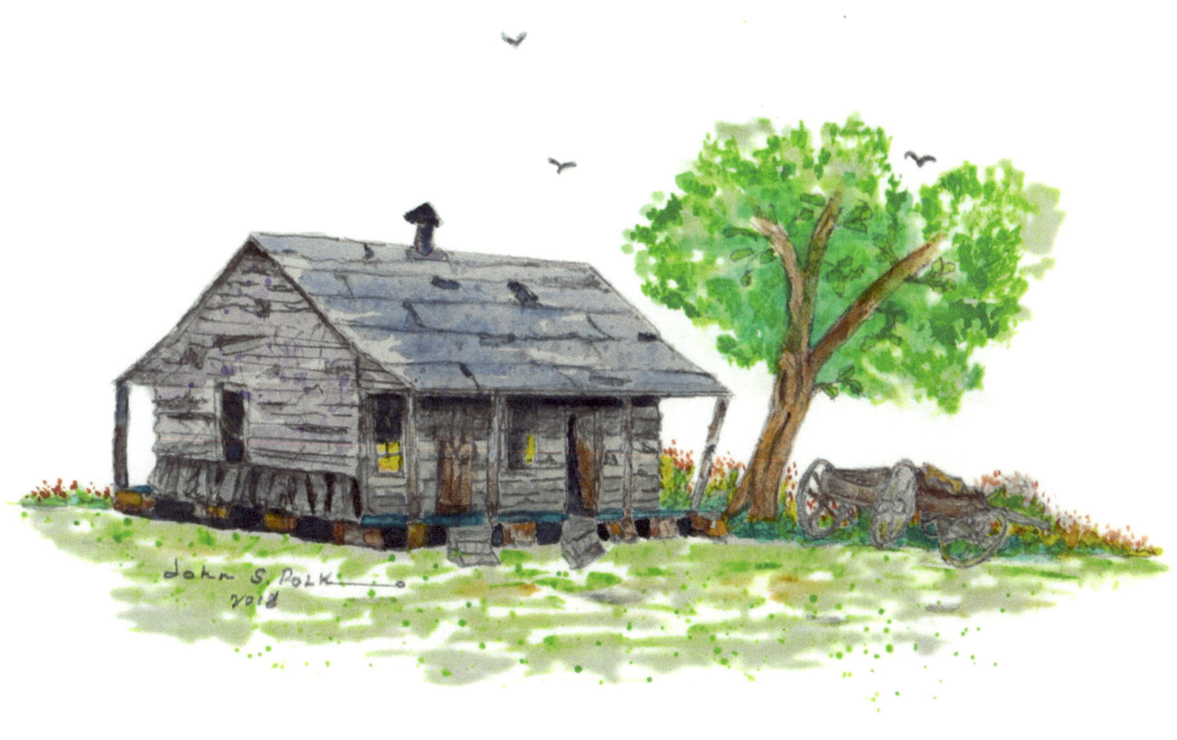

By Susan Polk Van Dusen

Art by John S. Polk

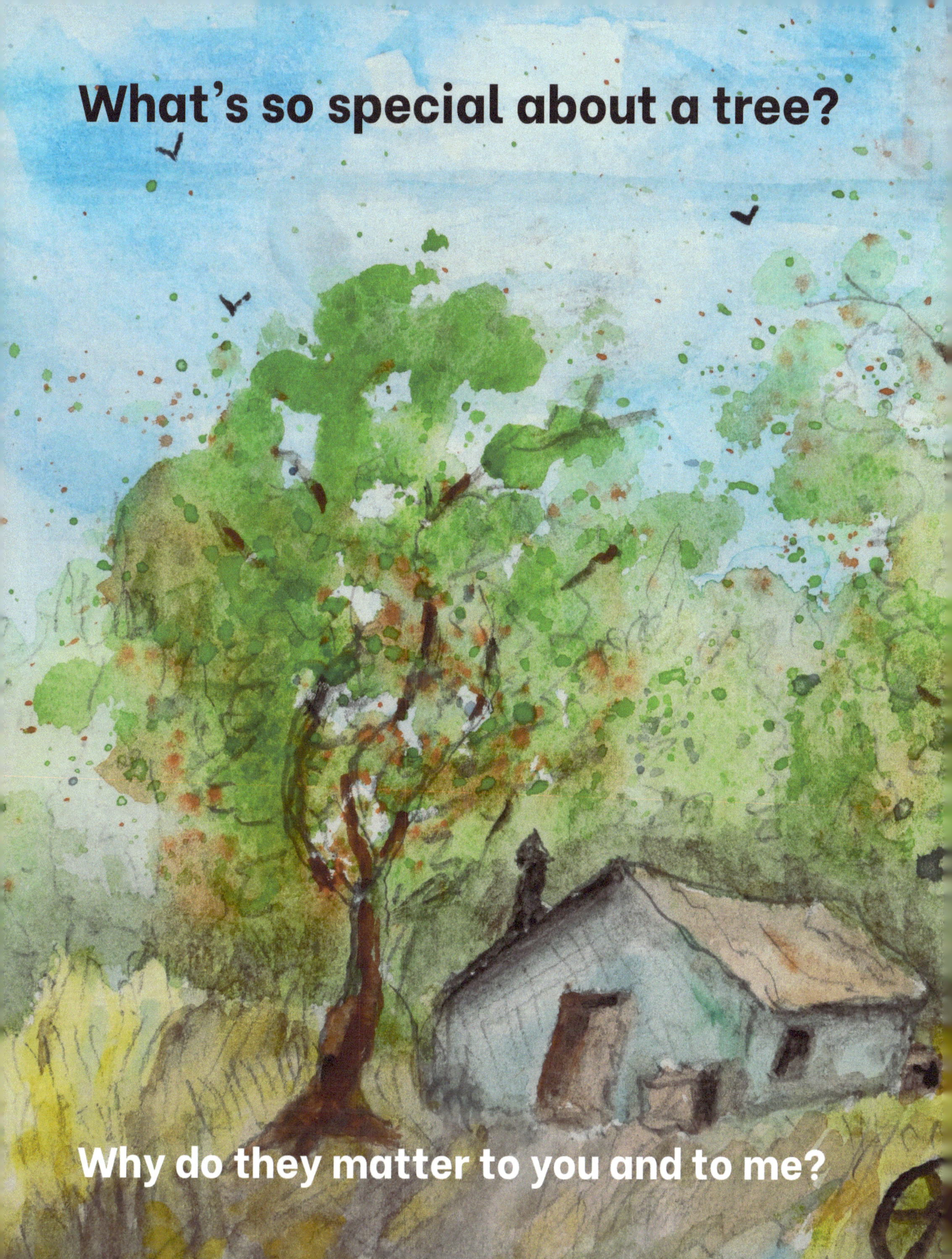
What's so special about a tree?
Why do they matter to you and to me?

Trees provide
shelter,
CLEAN AIR,
and shade.

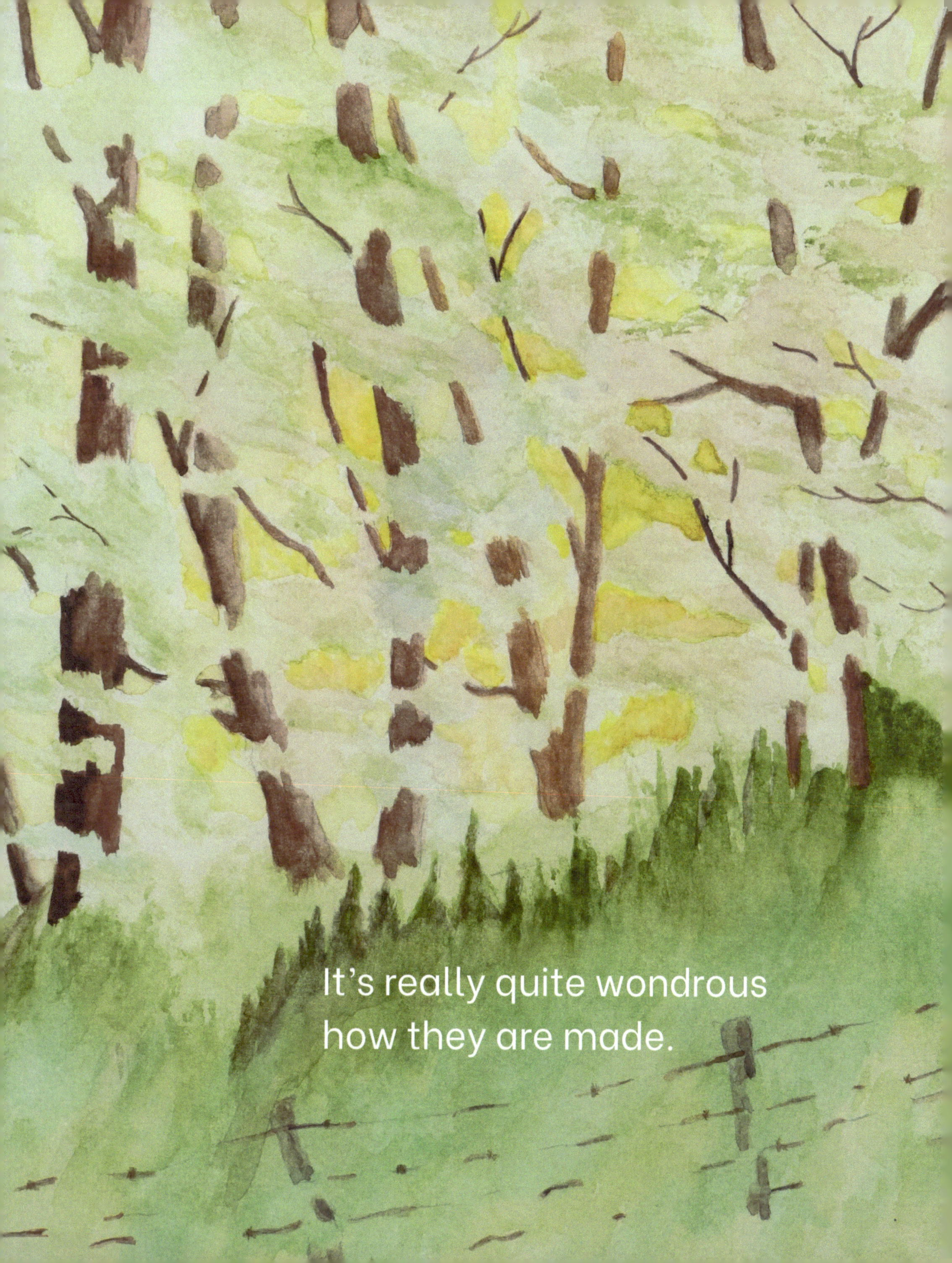
It's really quite wondrous
how they are made.

Some trees are TALL and
reach toward the SKY,

guarding the woodlands

for ALL who pass by.

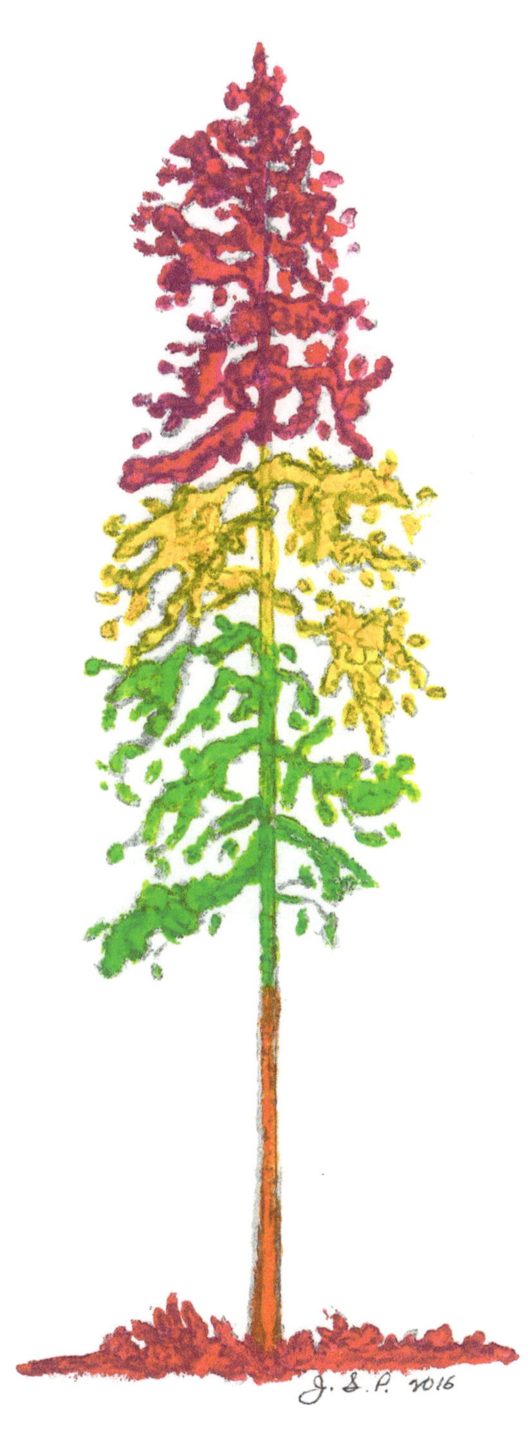

Some trees are **MIGHTY,** thick, heavy, and 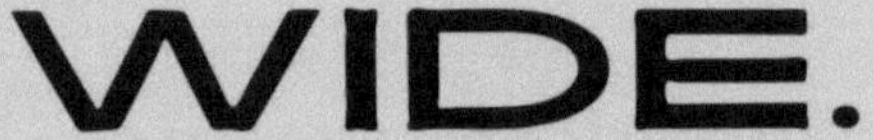

WIDE.

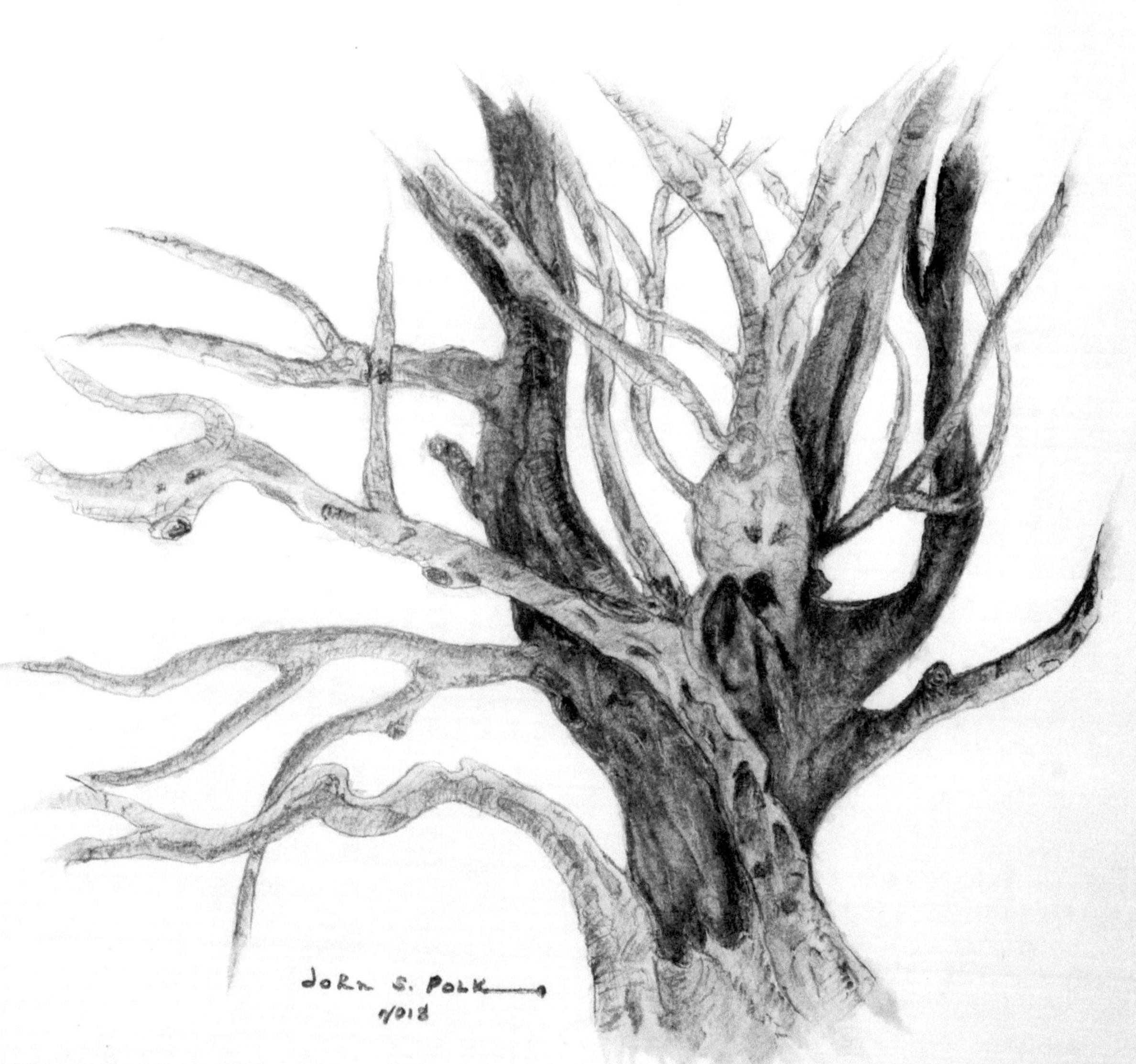
John S. Polk
1/018

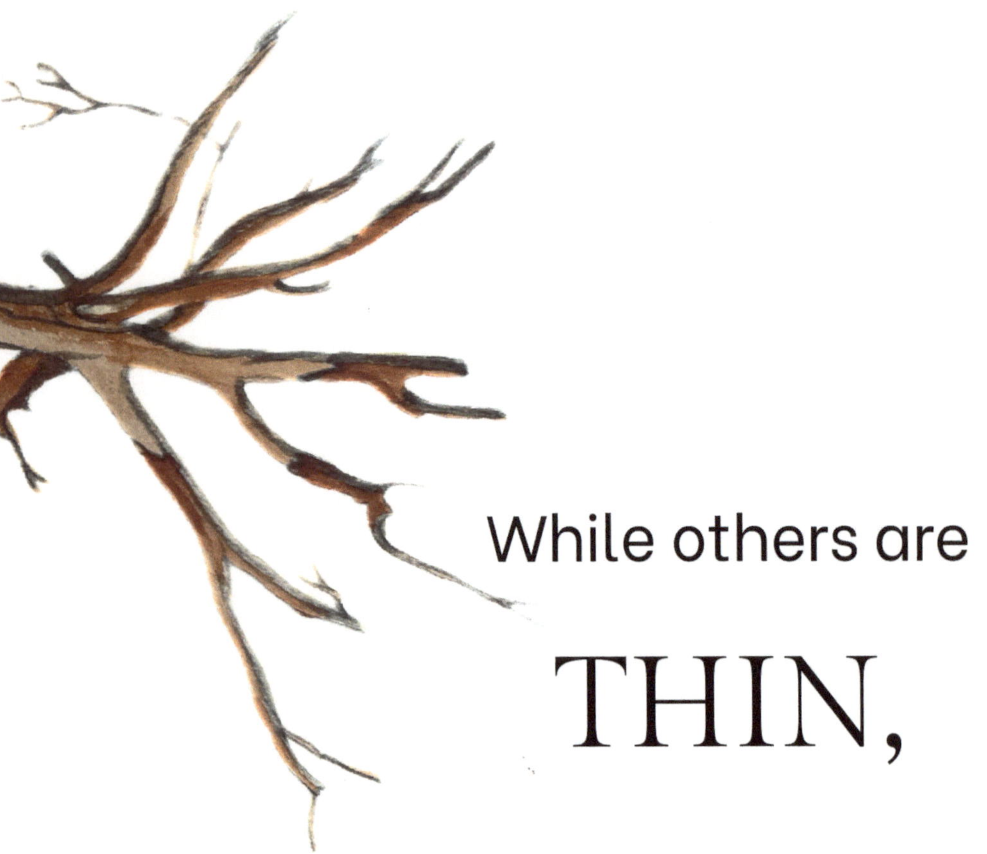

While others are

THIN,

branches bare on each side.

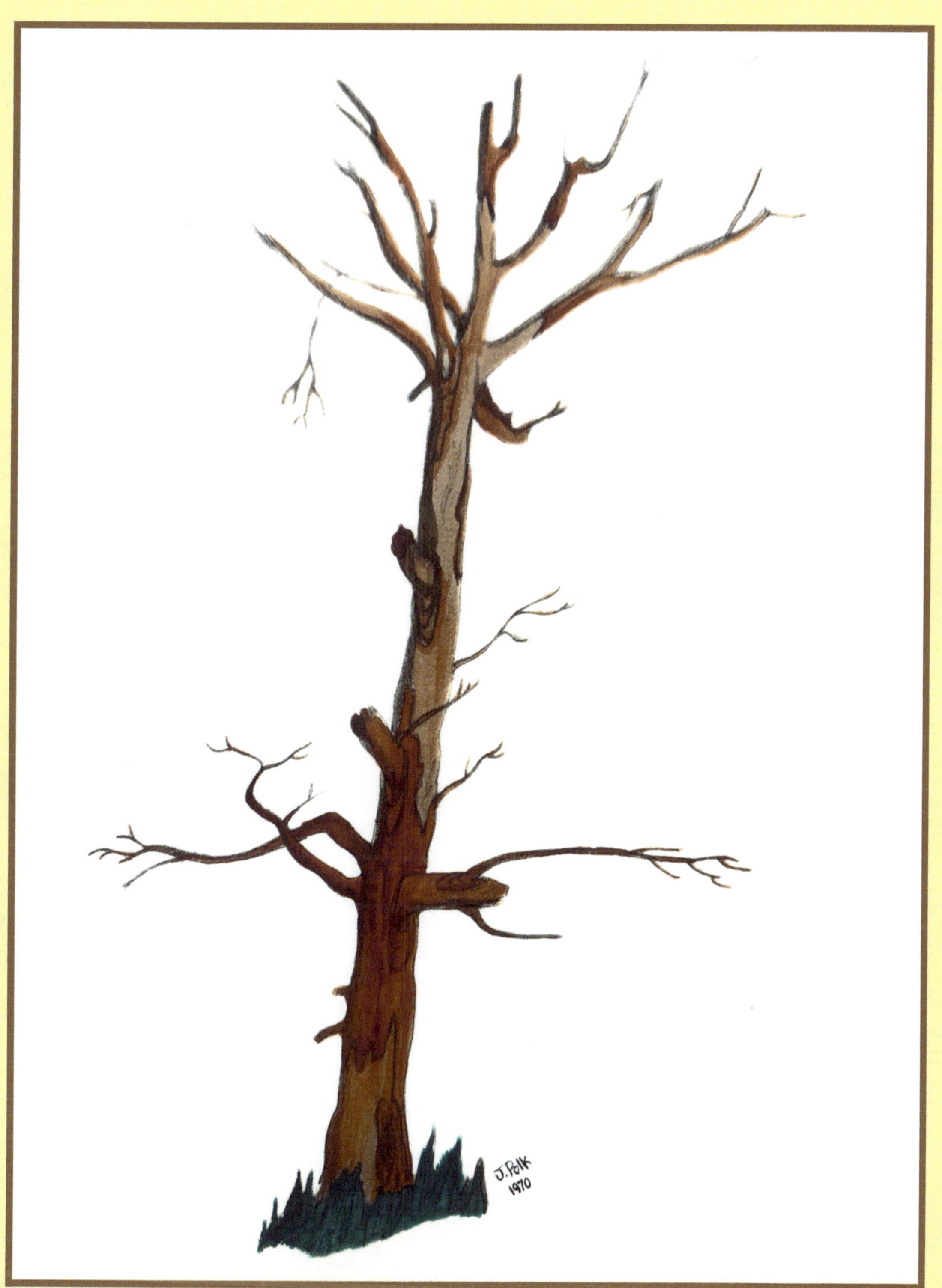

J. Polk
1970

Some spread their limbs

and seem to take FLIGHT.

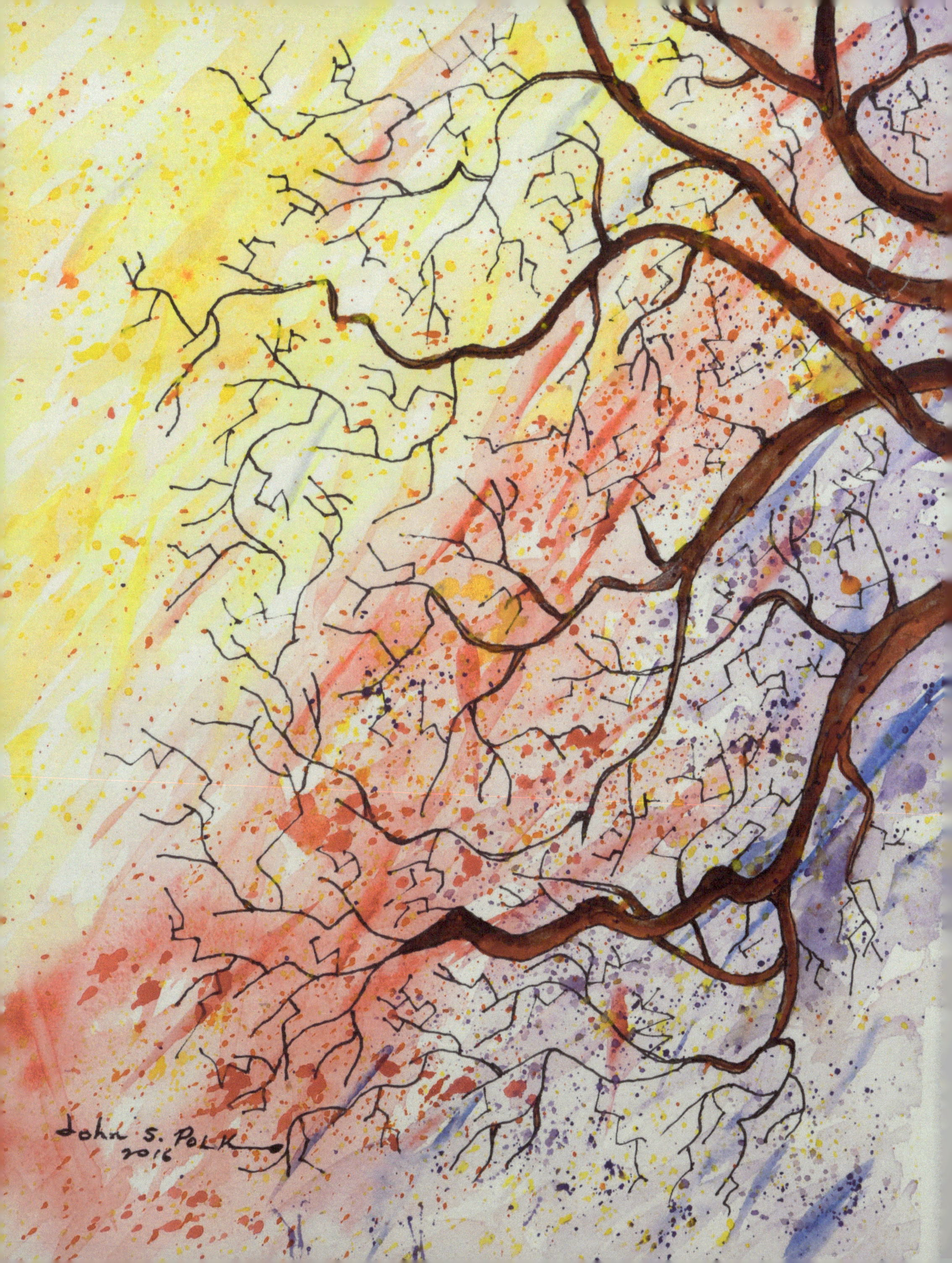

John S. Polk
2016

While others meet autumn

with **COLORS** so bright.

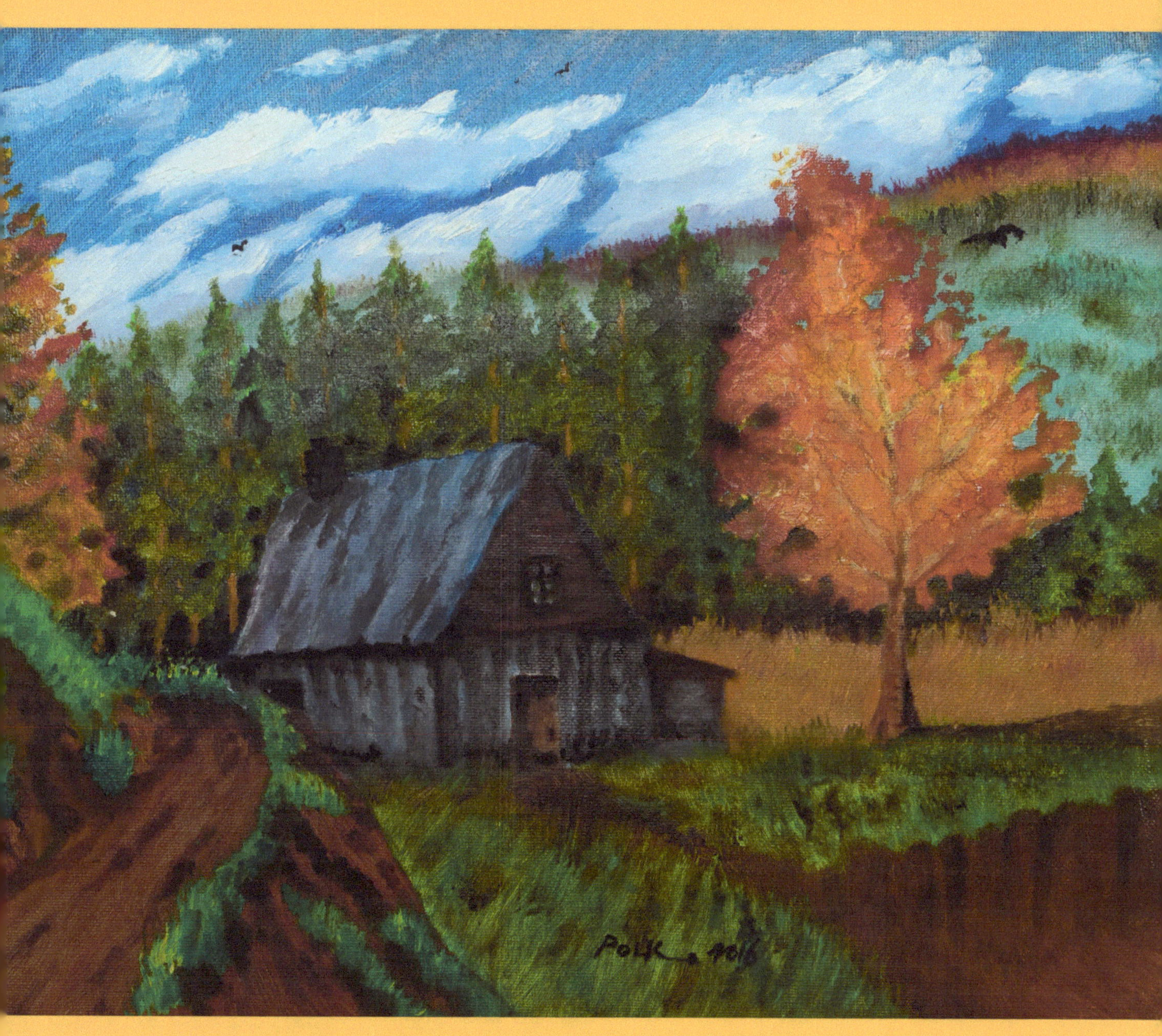

Some STAND in the forest —

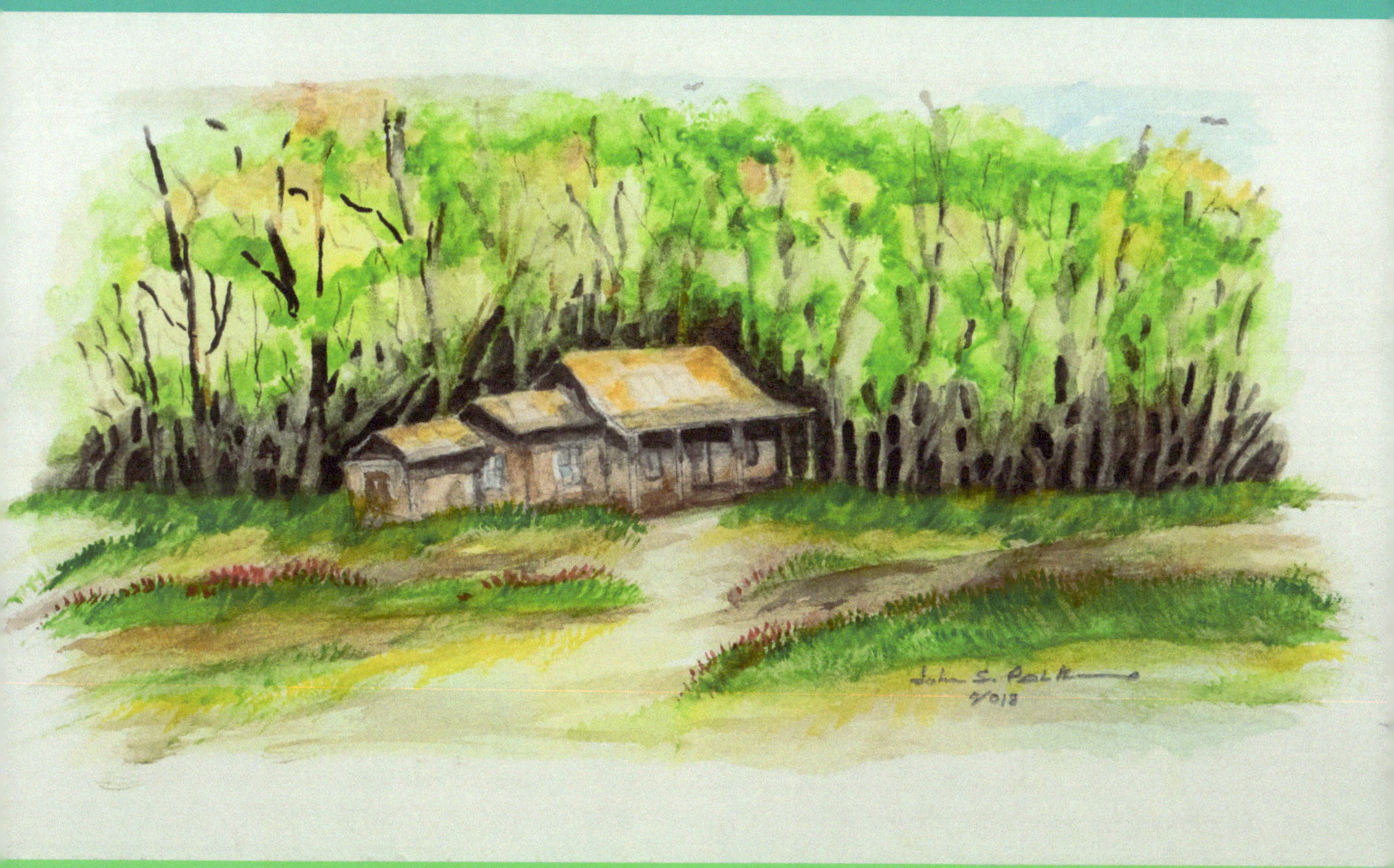

an **ARMY** of trees.

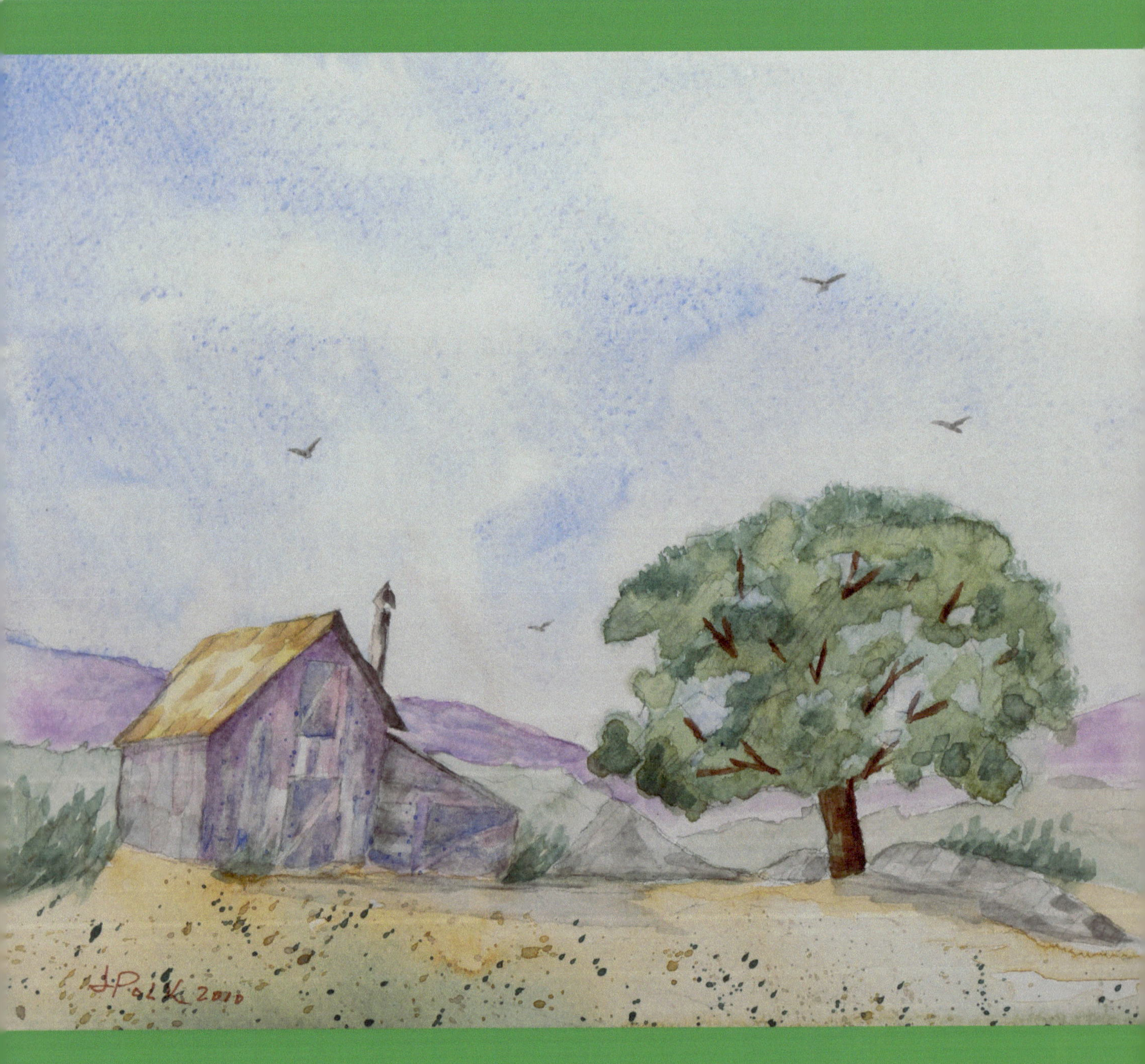

While some stand alone,
Swaying
slow in the breeze.

Some grow in the countryside,
tall,
full,
and GREEN.

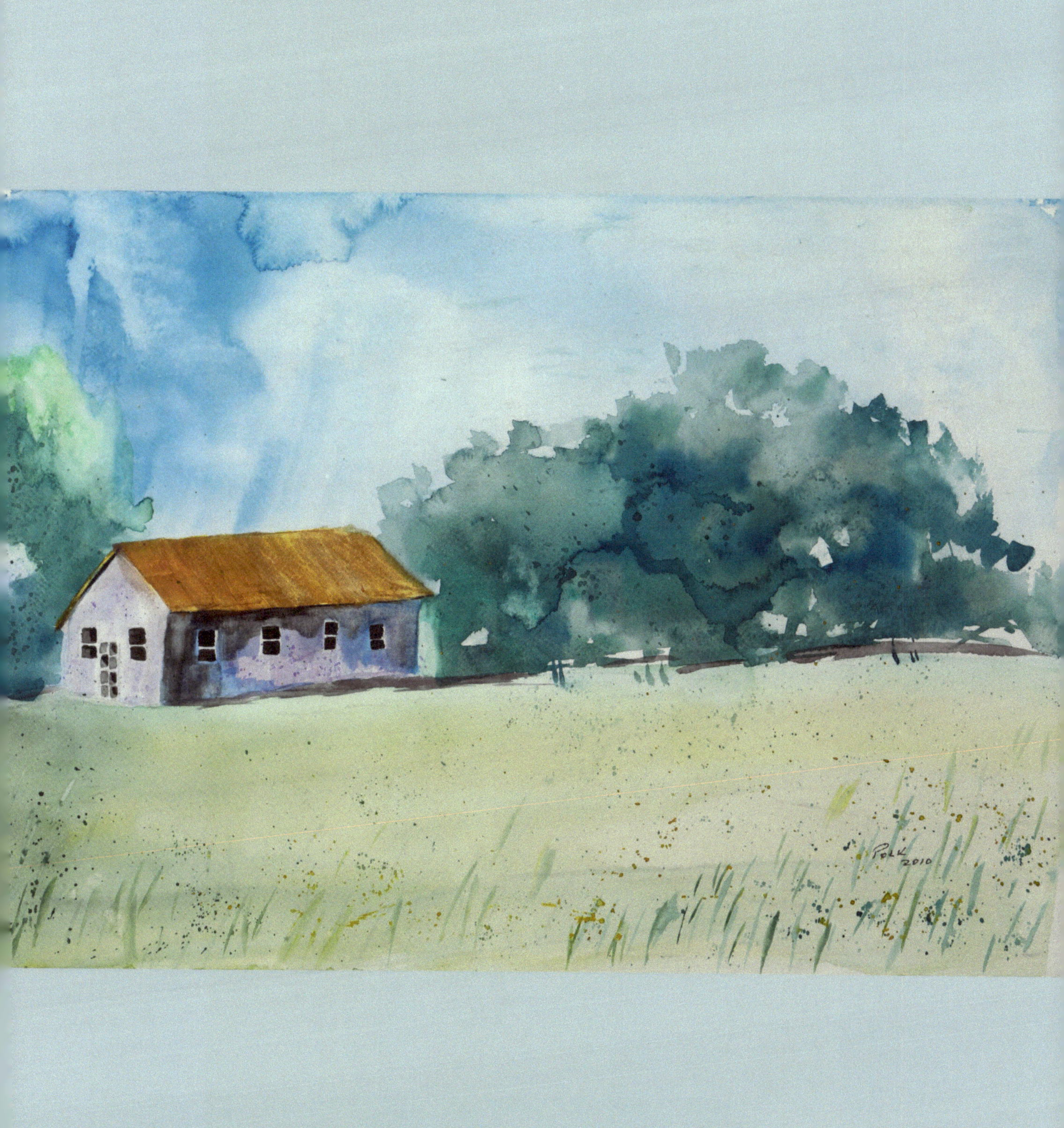

Polk
2010

While some guard the *RIVER*
with water serene.

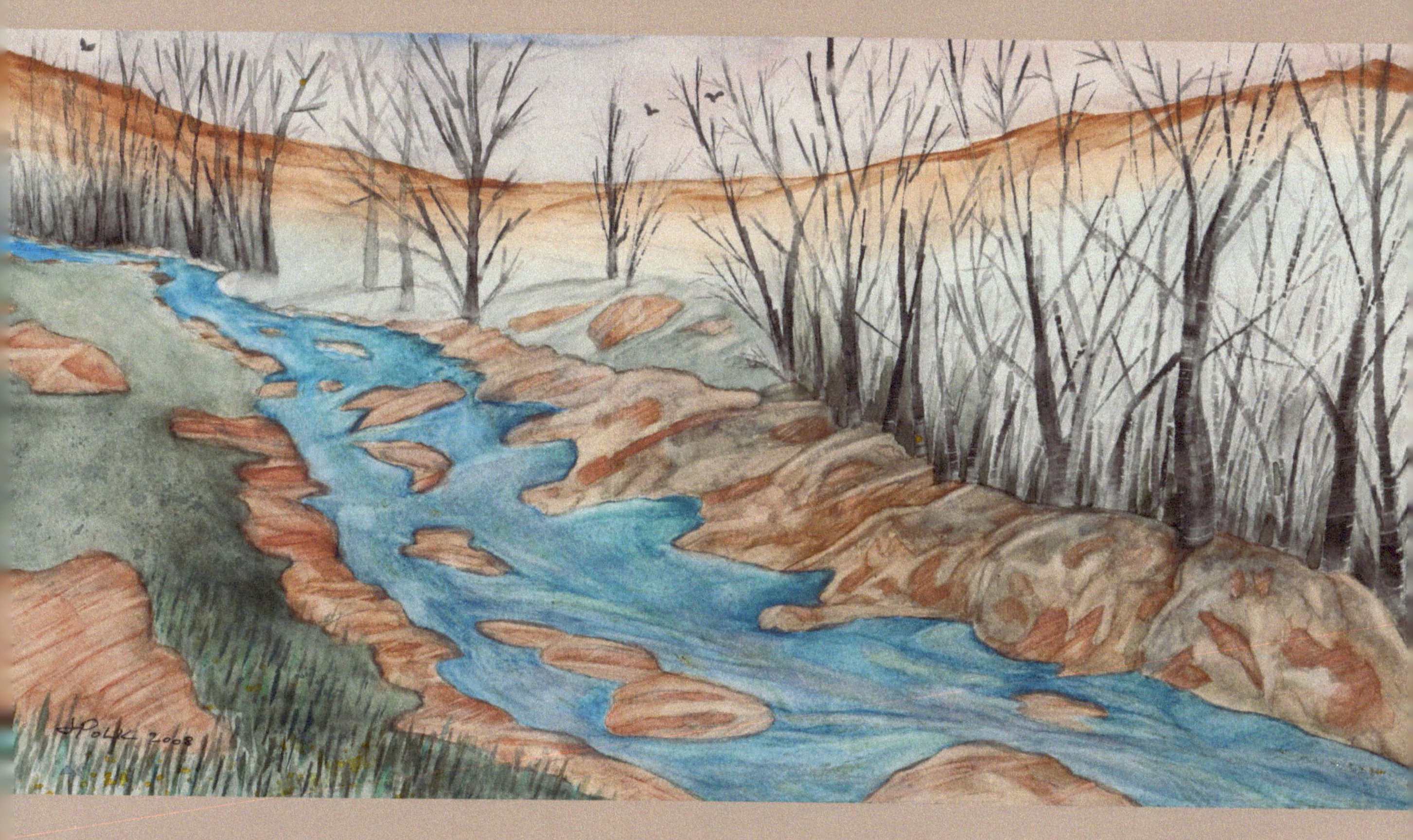
HPolk 2008

No one can tell a proud **TREE** what to do.

Its life is a **BLESSING** for me and for you.

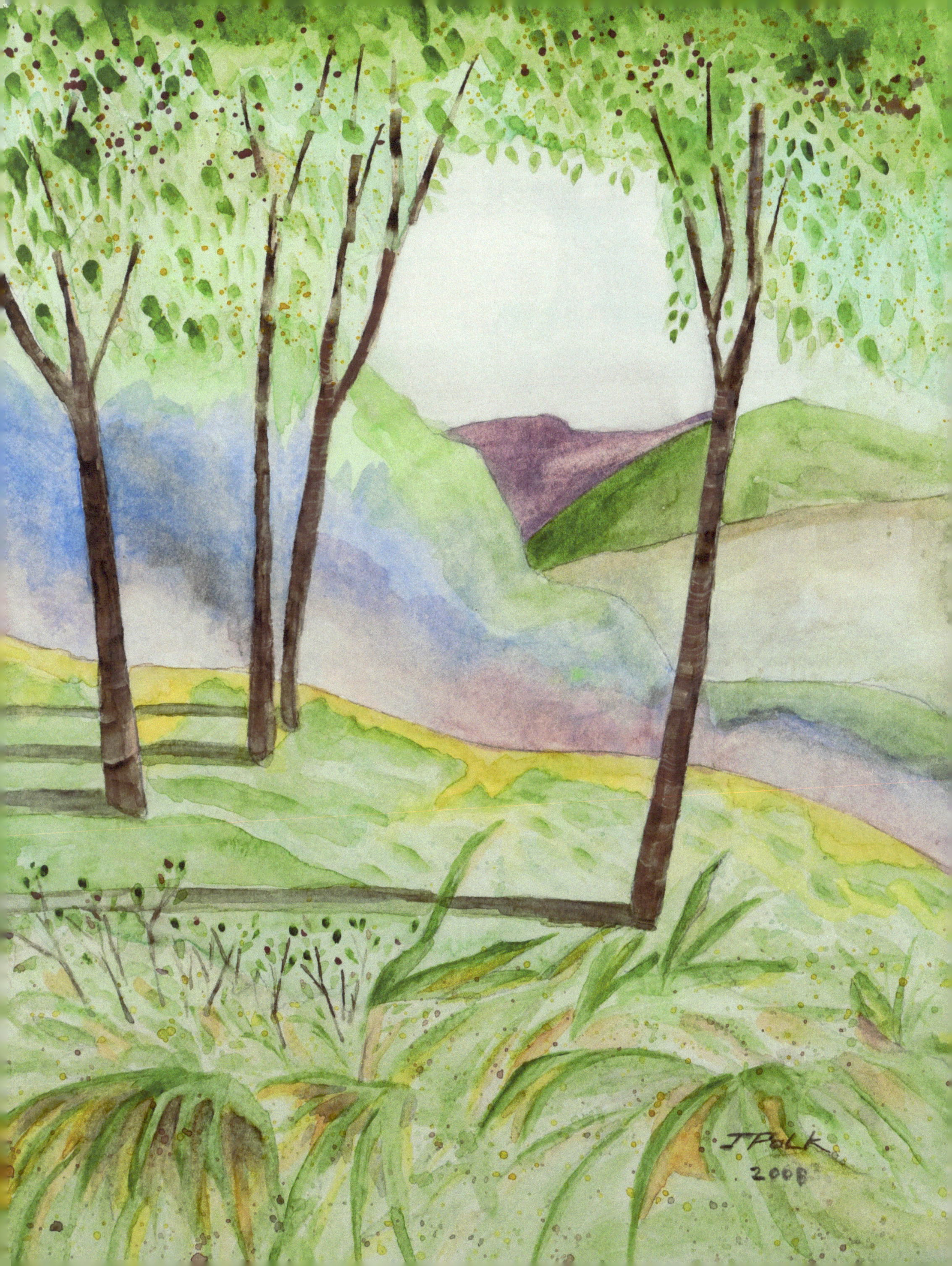

JPolk
2008

ARTWORK IN THIS BOOK

COVER: Rebirth on the Hill — pencil and watercolor on paper, 2017

In order of appearance:

Sharecropper's House, Arkansas Delta — pencil and watercolor on paper, 2018

Cottage in the Wood — pencil and watercolor on paper, 2017

Untitled — watercolor on paper, 2007

Lodgepole Tree — watercolor on paper, 2016

Untitled — pencil and watercolor on paper, 2018

Untitled — pencil and watercolor on paper, 1970

Blowing in the Wind — watercolor and ink on paper, 2016

Splendor in the Forest — oil paint on canvas board, 2016

Meadow by Woods — pencil and watercolor on paper, 2018

Untitled — watercolor on paper, 2010

Untitled — watercolor on paper, 2010

Untitled — watercolor on paper, 2008

Untitled — watercolor and pencil on paper, 2008

View more artwork by John S. Polk at polkfineart.pixels.com.

Author's Note

My dad, John S. Polk, was an extremely talented visual artist who showed artistic skill in his childhood but perfected his craft late in life. After he and my mom passed away, I inherited almost 400 of his paintings and drawings. These are in addition to dozens he gave away during his lifetime.

The idea to incorporate my dad's art into a picture book came to me in 2024. I chose trees as the theme, as he had multiple paintings depicting various types of trees, both realistic and fanciful. I wrote the book's text in a rhyming verse that gently ties together a selection of these beautiful paintings.

I think he would be proud of the end result and wish he were here to hold it in his hands.

Susan

About the Author

As a child, Susan Polk Van Dusen visited the library every week with her parents and brought home stacks of books to enjoy. After having kids of her own, Susan continued the tradition with weekly trips to library storytime and nightly bedtime stories. Now, she hopes her picture books will bring joy to countless children and the grownups who love them.

Susan has two grown daughters. She lives in Arkansas with her husband, Tim, their border collie, Sadie, and their dachshund, Bones. She is the daughter of this book's artist, John S. Polk.

About the Artist

John S. Polk was a visual artist based in Hot Springs, Arkansas, who worked primarily in watercolor, oil, and graphite. When John passed away in March 2020, he left an extensive collection of works across an array of subject matter including architecture, landscapes, pastoral scenes, and portraits of people from different ethnic and cultural backgrounds. He is the dad of this book's author, Susan Polk Van Dusen.